Love And Space Dust Volume II

- David Jones -

David Jones is an internationally best selling author living in Liverpool, UK. He has published both poetry and prose, and his books are known to explore the deeper feelings of life, emotions we have all felt and experiences we have all been through. People across the world identify strongly with his words and often find comfort within the pages of his books.

As well as writing and publishing books, David also writes scripts for theatre, acts and recently returned from a successful run as part of a comedy sketch troupe at the Edinburgh Festival. He also writes and directs short films, as well as uploading to his Youtube channel. David can be found on Facebook, Twitter @djthedavid, Instagram @storydj and on Youtube at youtube.com/storydj.

For more information on the writer, visit: https://storydj.wordpress.com/ or https://twitter.com/StoryDJay or on Facebook at https://www.facebook.com/davidjoneswriter.

"Soulmates always find each other. In space. In time. Through galaxies and cosmos. Soulmates always find each other."

It will hurt

And hurt
And hurt

And then
One day

It won't.

There's nothing
Louder,
Than the
Silence

Between
Two people
Who used

To love
Each other.

I don't
Know why,
But I still
Believe
It will be

You and I.

3 risks you have to take in life

1. Trust love one more time.
2. Open up again after getting hurt.
3. Tell them how you feel.

I didn't ask,
Because I was
Afraid

Of the
Answer.

And the
Hardest lesson
To learn,

Is how
To be alone
All over

Again.

"But life went on."

- *A 4 word short story.*

I miss
The stars
You put
In my
Sky.

All the stars
In the night sky
And here
I am

wishing for you.

I fell in love

With the galaxies

That shine

In your

Eyes.

You are

The star I search for

Whenever I look

Into the night

Sky.

I wonder how many lives
I'll have to live, until I
Find my way back
To you.

You are
Every star I've
Ever wished
Upon

And every dream
I've ever
Dreamed.

I spent

Too long waiting

For words

You'd never

Say.

To feel
This way and
Say nothing

Is the worst
Pain of
All.

The 3 loudest types of silence

1. The silence between two ex lovers.
2. The silence of loving someone but never telling them.
3. The silence when words run out.

The hardest
Time to say goodbye,
Is when you
Have to, but

Don't want
To.

I wanted
So much to
Speak to you,

But I kept
Quiet.

When to
Hold on.

When to
Let go.

Two lessons,
So hard to
Learn.

The end
Of us will not
Be the end

Of me.

3 of the most important journeys

1. From love, to hurt, to trusting love again.
2. From regretting your decisions, to forgiving yourself.
3. From trying to be who people expect you to be, to being yourself.

In the end,
All I learned was
How to love
Somebody,

Even if you can't
Be with
Them.

Two things
I'll never forget:

The way you
Looked at me for
The first time

And the
Last time.

"We're different people now, so I hope we can meet again for the first time."

I spend
My nights
Dreaming of
You

And my
Mornings
Waking up
Without

you.

The night sky
Shines

With all my
Memories of

You.

I looked up
At the stars and it
Hurt a little less.

3 lessons we can learn from the stars

1. The darker the night, the brighter they shine.
2. No matter how lost you feel, there's always a light to guide you home.
3. They end, but only to begin again.

There will
Always be something
Between us.

Whenever I look up
At the moon
And the stars,

I'll think
Of you.

To be with you,
Just once more
Beneath
The stars.

I swear
That would be
Enough.

Things change.

Sometimes
It hurts.

Sometimes
It hurts
A lot.

Sometimes it's
For the best.

The worst goodbye
Is the one you
Never thought
You'd have to say.

When it's over,
It's the happy memories
That hurt.

To see
Your face and
Feel nothing,

That would be
Peace at
Last.

Some people

Can be in your memories

But not

Your life.

"Two soulmates who didn't find each other."

An 8 word short story.

You might
Have to begin again
More than
Once.

3 things to stop waiting for

1. For them to message back.
2. For them to come back, long after
they've gone.
3. For them to give back the love you
gave.

"The hardest thing in life is finding somebody you can't live without, and then living without them."

And
Life went
On.

It was not
The same,

But it
Went on.

Perhaps
I wanted you
To fight
For me,
The way I

Would have
Fought for
You.

Imagine
Being happy.

No ifs,
No buts,
Just
Happy.

I suppose
I'll just keep loving
You, until

One day

It ends.

But I
Fell in love
With an

Impossibility.

The memories
That hurt the most,
Teach the most.

Let go,
And see
If they

Hold
On.

"You say you want to let go, but deep down you're scared. Deep down you want to hold on, even though you know it's killing you."

You are

The space dust

In my

Soul.

"I wait for you at sunset. When the world goes to sleep, I know I'll find you in my dreams."

Perhaps
The person
I really
Miss,

Is who I
Thought you
Were.

And it will
Hurt, until it doesn't
Anymore.

I keep trying
To find you
In other
People.

Time moves
Slower when you
Miss somebody.

"And my story goes on, without you."

A 7 word short story.

Oh how
We break, when
There's nobody
Around to
See.

What hurts
Today,
Teaches
Tomorrow.

"I just wanted to tell you, I love you. I love you so much. I don't know when it happened, or even why. I don't expect anything back. You don't even need to reply. I just wanted to tell you that I love you."

Messages I'll never send.

I wish it had
Meant as little to me,
As it did
To you.

How sad
To miss someone,
Who you know
Doesn't miss
You.

"We were almost a story."

A 5 word short story.

How sad
To face the future,
Without the one
You planned
It with.

"Despite everything, I'm glad we met."

A 6 word short story.

It was
That smile.

The first time
I saw it, I knew
I wanted to see it
For the rest

Of my life.

"Heartbroken over a love that didn't even exist."

An 8 word short story.

"I pretend it doesn't bother me, but it's tearing me apart."

"And sometimes it surprises you. How much it hurts. Still. After all this time. Here. Now. Like this. But it still hurts."

"We'll pass each other on the street in a few year's time. We won't stop, but I know I'll smile."

I hope
There's another life
And can try
Again.

One day
The sadness will
Be just a
Memory.

Missing them
Isn't the same
As loving

them.

It hurts,
When the person
Who is your
First priority

Makes you
Their
Last.

Time

Goes by and you

Miss them

A little

Less.

To love

Her is to wish

Upon strange

Stars.

I choose
To believe, that
Some people

Meet for
A reason.

"I miss you" said the moon, but the stars were far away and only silence answered.

How sad
To dream of you,
But wake up
Without you.

There's no
Easy way to say
Goodbye

To the one
You love.

"I choose to believe that even death isn't the end, and we'll seek each other out amongst the stars."

You lose
A part of yourself,
When you lose
Somebody
You love.

There's nothing
More difficult than trying
To forget someone
You love.

You were
The love that felt
Like home.

"I still check my phone and expect to see a message from you."

Nothing hurts
More than

What might
Have been.

I hope
We can find
Forever
Again.

How could I
Forget you?

You gave me
So much to
Remember.

You were the
Love I dreamed of,
Before I even
Knew

Who you
Were.

"You are worth the stars, the suns and the galaxies: all the space dust in your soul."

The Undead Astronaut

"Be careful what you wish for."

The Undead Astronaut takes a seat at the kitchen table cracks open a bottle of whisky pours himself a glass - *no ice* - straight down the hatch.

"I didn't wish for you" says the little girl "I was seriously hoping for someone better."

"But you wished upon my star. The cold dead ugly one that people tend to neglect. You're the first one that's actually made a wish on it. Unbelievable."

He lifts his visor but keeps the helmet on, threads another whisky through the gap - *down it goes* - reaches for the bottle again - *I think I'm owed at least another three* - and down they go as well. The girl tells him to slow down but the Undead Astronaut has come a long way and, quite frankly, been through quite a lot since the days when he was simply The Astronaut, carefree and in love and eager to get back to earth and live happily ever after.

In the end he picks up the entire bottle, drinks it and passes out where he sits.

"Well" says the girl "This isn't what I expected but I suppose it's better than nothing and will have to do."

She lets him sleep and finds him the next morning, still slumped over the table in his full astronaut uniform, oxygen pack and all. Snores echo cavernous inside his helmet. She prods him. Shoves him. Finally kicks him in the shin.

"Mr Undead Astronaut?" she asks tentatively as he wakes up in a flurry of swearing.

"Yes? What is it? My head's splitting open…"

"Maybe you'd feel better if you took your helmet off?"

"Can't do that. Can't be sure of the air."

"But aren't you human, Mr Undead Astronaut sir, and don't we all breathe the same air?"

The Undead Astronaut gets to his feet and pats himself down as if he's checking that he's still here. The business of the dead star and the solitary wish has shaken him up. Earth used to be his home but he's been to the furthest fringes of the universe, to the end and (nearly) the beginning of time. All the Undead Astronaut can do is hope and search. That, in the end, is his only purpose, miserable as it is.

The girl stands a little distance away with her arms folded. When that doesn't work she starts tapping her foot and then lets out the odd theatrical sigh.

"What?" asks the Undead Astronaut at last.

"My wish."

"What was it?"

"Don't you write them down?"

"It's hard to keep track."

"I thought nobody wished on your star?"

"That's why I stopped listening. You got lucky."

He can tell that she feels anything but. When people wish upon stars they hope for dramatic interventions. The last thing they expect is the Undead Astronaut, bitter and sad and drunk and now hungover. But that's the fault of people for making wishes and expecting them to come true, just as if the universe owes anybody anything.

"My wish" she says "Was to find out what's over the horizon."

The Undead Astronaut sways, is nearly sick, and sits down again.

"Well that's easy enough" he says after a moment's consideration "Have you got a car?"

"You don't understand. Whenever I go anywhere there's just another horizon, and then I want to know what's on the other side of that."

The predicament dawns slowly and then all at once. The Undead Astronaut realises the scale of the problem and see's that it's going to take a lot more effort than he'd like. All the while she just stands there, tapping her foot and sighing. He could have coped with waterworks. It's a long time since the Undead Astronaut felt anything even resembling sentiment, especially towards children. If she'd only cry he could pick up his oxygen pack in disgust and storm out.

Instead she just looks disappointed and the Undead Astronaut realises that - *if we're going to be really serious about this whole business* - he must be the biggest disappointment in the world. It crosses his mind again. What people expect when they wish upon stars. Children want angels or Little Princes to descend in a sea of white light, granting their wishes in a flurry of magic and celestial music. The Undead Astronaut feels sick and hungover. He's even eyeing up the route to the bathroom.

For a moment he's tired of himself - *who he is, was and will be* - all of it. The Undead Astronaut.

"Alright" he says, staggering to his feet "You wished on the wrong star but I'm a man of my word. Let's have a look at that horizon. We'll take the bus."

The driver lets them on, but when they take their seats at the back it's all stares and the Undead Astronaut, still in his space suit, visor down and even carrying his oxygen tank, stands out obtuse and absurd: a sad spectacle for a sad time. He persists with these precautions even though they're no longer necessary. They remind him of a time when he was simply an astronaut with a family and a life and a love waiting for him at home, long before he was left to drift through spacetime. He tries to find his way back - has come close - sometimes even painfully close - but never quite close enough.

"Mr Undead Astronaut?" asks the girl "Where are we going?"

The Undead Astronaut squints through the window as the houses and the shops parade by. They're sliding through the suburbs, some of it recognisable from light years ago. Half memories pass through his thoughts, dulled by the passage of time. Since those days he's sat down with kings and he's broken bread with conquerors. On the eve of Alesia, Cesar told him that love is nothing, and only history matters. Hannibal told him something similar just before Canae. He sat with Roland and Charlemagne as they laughed together just before Roncevaux. To be an immortal name. But the Undead Astronaut knows that there is no history, not really. In time it all fades, and only experiences, memories, stay. Only love is infinite, and more's the pity.

"I checked the route map" he replies at last "We're going to the highest point in the city. We'll get a proper look at that horizon you're so worried about."

"But -" begins the girl.

"You think I don't know what I'm doing? I've got my own star. It's a bit beat up, but what have you got?"

The rest of the journey passes in silence and the passengers, much too anaesthetised - *the process of every day life day in day out ad infinitum* - to make any comments, soon forget about him.

Groggy from his whisky induced sleep, the Undead Astronaut misjudges the stops and they end up having to walk through a shopping mall. He trudges in his heavy space boots and suit, tugging at his collar in the heat. When they pass a television store the girl insists that they go in. She strolls between the big screens transfixed on rainforests and seashores and deep jungles. The Undead Astronaut has seen it all and more, of course. He's even seen planets where three suns orbit in unison, it's always Tuesday and they celebrate everybody's birthday at once on the 78th Tuesday of the year.

He notices a gigantic curved television showing a space movie. The Undead Astronaut pauses. Doesn't feel anything even resembling sentiment at the sight of the shuttle or the capsule. All he sees are errors and inaccuracies and absurdities. He's so riveted on the screen and busy pointing out the mistakes to anyone who'll listen that he loses sight of the girl completely. He doesn't even notice that she's gone until a salesman asks him if he didn't come in with a child.

"What?" says the Undead Astronaut, still irate about the ridiculous way they're portraying zero gravity.

"A kid? You had a kid with you when you came in. I noticed because we've never had an astronaut look at the televisions before."

"Oh no" says the Undead Astronaut, and dashes outside as fast as his space boots will allow.

He pushes and curses his way through the shopper crowd, which seems to have grown exponentially now that he's in a hurry. The faceless masses mumble and complain, the odd elbow connects with his space suit and there's even an upset shopping trolley, but in the end he finds her sat quite placidly in a cafe, kicking her legs as though she doesn't have a care in the world.

"Don't wander off" he says, trying not to sound as if he cares.

"I thought you'd be pleased to get rid of me."

The Undead Astronaut shrugs and tells her that if he lost her now, the whole business with the wish would go unfinished. Although the universe isn't big on consequence and barely has cause and effect in anything like the way people understand it, he personally doesn't like loose ends. There's only ever been one and it looms over him like a spectre. Words he could - *should* - have said. A love he should never have left behind. That's the crux of it. He should have stayed. Really when you think about it - *better not to think about it.*

"You looked warm" continues the girl "So I got you a cold drink. And a straw for your helmet."

She hands him an iced drink with a long, pink straw that he manages to thread through his visor. It's been a long time since the Undead Astronaut tasted anything that isn't space rations or potent liquor. The sucrose flavour of the drink restores his senses.

"Thanks."

"It's ok" but she eyes him strangely, as though she has another question that she's reluctant to ask.

"Out with it" says the Undead Astronaut.

"I wondered…did you used to live on Earth, before you became an astronaut?"

"I used to live in a house not far from here, probably less than a hundred years before you were born. I was happy."

"Aren't you happy now, Mr Undead Astronaut?"

"Do I look happy to you!?" and then more kindly "I don't have a home. Nobody can be happy without a home. Even if they wander a long way, even if they don't go back to their home very often…just having one is enough to be happy."

"But you do have a home" she persists "You just told me."

"I can't get back there. That's what I've been trying to do. Find my way back."

"But it's still your home. So it isn't gone. You're just a long way from it. Next time I see your star I'll wish for you to go home. Do you think that will work?"

As if I haven't thought of that myself a million times before thinks the Undead Astronaut but he just shrugs.

"Anything's possible."

They sit in silence for a few moments. One of the loudspeakers plays a jaunty tune, the latest bit of popular music, and the Undead Astronaut suggests that they better get moving if they want to sort out the horizon wish before nightfall.

"I think we should take a different route" says the girl as they get up to leave.

"You know the way?"

"We got on the wrong bus. I didn't like to say."

The Undead Astronaut breathes a sigh of relief when they reach the hillside. A cool breeze whips around his legs and, save for the distant murmur of traffic far below, it's the closest he's come to peace and quiet since he arrived back on earth. The view of the horizon unfolds like a painting. Hills and woodland and the city limits and then a radio tower and a cloud bank merging into obscurity.

"You see" the Undead Astronaut says as they stand side by side, gazing out "That's the horizon."

"I know what the horizon is. What I want to know is what comes after it."

"Another one" replies the Undead Astronaut.

"And then?"

"Another one."

"There must be a final one. I want to know what's over the very last horizon."

"There isn't" the Undead Astronaut raises a gloved hand against the sun "There are just more horizons. That's the sublime beauty and the appalling nightmare of it. No matter how far you go, there's always more, and then even more."

A dog walker passes by, nods and says good afternoon. The dog tugs on its lead, sniffs at the Undead Astronaut's oxygen pack, but they're quickly on their way.

"You don't want to know what's over the horizon" he continues "Not really. What you want to know is why there are so many, and what the point of them is. The Earth is round…"

"I know that."

"So if you go all the way around it in a perfectly straight line you'll come back to where you were."

"What, that's it? All those horizons and you just come back to the same spot?"

The Undead Astronaut thinks about it. Squints through the sun towards the radio tower the hills beyond the nimbus clouds bubbling in the furthest reaches.

"But you're not the same person. You've seen so much and been to so many places that you're completely different. You might stand on the same spot again, but it's not the same you that left. That's the point of the horizons. Every one of them makes a new you."

They stand side by side for a few moments and the Undead Astronaut feels pretty good about himself. The statement about the new yous came suddenly and without warning, a genuine flash of inspiration amongst an otherwise uninspired life of cynicism made all the more bitter by everything that he's seen. Galaxies colliding. Entire nebula gobbled into the hungry hearts of black holes. Satellites orbiting cold dead suns at the very end where all the people do is throw parties the stars gone out one by one nothing left and everybody getting drunk and pretending that there's hope or rebirth or more chances to come…

"I have another question" says the girl.

I hate kids thinks the Undead Astronaut, although he doesn't really mean it.

"Ask away."

"What about space. The stars. If you keep going will you still come back to yourself?"

Now that's the million dollar question. The Undead Astronaut has been searching. Waiting. Drifting. Spacetime contorts, it's unpredictable. He's been clinging onto the hope that if he simply goes on living he'll eventually find his way back to his old life, and the love who he still dreams of, even though there are aeons between them. So far, so lousy, and no such luck. He raises his visor and feels the warmth of the Earth sun on his face. It's familiar, even comforting, like coming home and closing the door behind you on a cold winter's night.

"The universe might be infinite. Probably is" it naturally follows "So it goes on forever. Everything has happened and will happen again."

"So that means…" she pauses "That there are an infinite number of yous. That they go on forever too."

"I suppose it does."

Her eyes widen with the possibilities. All those maybes, those beginnings and those endless roads. The Undead Astronaut can tell that he's made an impact, but he's inadvertently made one on himself in the process. The sun on his face. Even the smell of the Earth breeze. The texture of it. He's almost back there. Once upon a time they walked up this hill and watched as the city lights blinked on one by one, the distant whir of traffic glowing along the highways.

So long ago now. More than infinity. To be home and in love. To watch the stars and the planets and feel the almighty cosmos move around you but to be in a single spot amongst it all and not need anything - *not a single thing* - apart from the person by your side. To have it all, to have more than the stars and the galaxies. And then to lose it.

"You know they terraform Jupiter one day?" says the Undead Astronaut quietly "They blast the gas away so that only the rocky core is left. Build cities in the clouds over Venus. And then further. Further out still. To Andromeda and then out to Centaurus A. Further. To planets where there are eight suns, a day lasts half an hour and everybody dances on the diamond shores on the fourteenth day of the fourteenth month. Planets where it rains erbium where the sea is quartz where time ticks backwards where the people remember the future not the past where black holes fill the horizon the atomised truth of everything the very end and perhaps the very beginning all over again…"

The Undead Astronaut rambles on but the girl isn't listening. Her eyes are fixed on the radio tower, the hills, the horizon and beyond, into the open road of possibility. Her life, and everything that it might be.

That evening, the Undead Astronaut returns to the hillside alone, through rush hour traffic and zigzagging pedestrians. They're all in too much of a hurry to notice him, and the whole world passes by as though it belongs to somebody else. The Undead Astronaut dares not hope. Once upon a time. He labours back up the hill, moaning and groaning in his spaceman attire the visor still down more as a matter of principle more than anything else. They used to sit here, side by side, the two of them, watching the city lights come on.

Everything was different back then. There was so much he hadn't seen, so much he didn't understand. He misses his old life, his innocence: being a fool who knew nothing about anything and didn't really need to. It's the nothing days. Days sat in front of the television. Walks through the park as the leaves turn brown. The dull fuzz of the radio in the morning. To be in love on a nothing day is to have the world and more.

"What about my wish?" he asks as the stars emerge slowly from the celestial soup but nothing, comes the answer, just like always.

In another life another time another universe another reality. The city lights flicker on one by one with the dusk, like a thousand glassy eyes. Traffic snakes this way and that, so far away as to be silent. He can almost feel her. She's almost next to him. The Undead Astronaut has stood witness to aeons. What are a few decades in the grand scheme of things and he does something that he's never done before - wishes - *even prays* - for mercy from the cruel heart of it - unfeeling reality - just a few decades - that she might appear, that time will do him some kind of favour.

Silence, comes the answer, just like always. Wind ruffles softly through the branches and a few roosting birds settle down. It must be autumn on Earth, because the night came on quickly and it's nearly fully dark, a web of lights beneath him. Who knows where he'll be tomorrow amongst the infinite cosmos. Maybe a little girl's wish will come good after all and send him back to his home. Or maybe he'll drift, through space and time, hoping against hope that in infinity he'll find his home again. It dawns on him slowly. Infinite potential. It's almost a comfort: maybe maybe maybe.

The whole jumble of stars and galaxies and black holes and nebula the very fabric of reality is all build upon a single word: *maybe*.

End.

More About the Author.

David Jones is an internationally best selling author living in Liverpool, UK. He has published both poetry and prose, and his books are known to explore the deeper feelings of life, emotions we have all felt and experiences we have all been through. People across the world identify strongly with his words and often find comfort within the pages of his books.

His poetry books have enjoyed tremendous success, often ranking as best sellers across the world. He has enjoyed a great deal of popularity on social media, and his writing has variously been posted by celebrities including Cara Delevingne, Khloe Kardashian, Britney Spears and Camilla Cabelo. He has also worked on academic projects and is currently completing a thesis in Early Modern travel writing at the University of Liverpool. His writing has been greeted with critical acclaim, and he is currently working on a full, feature length novel exploring themes of love, eternity, the nature of the universe and history.

As well as writing and publishing books, David also writes scripts for theatre, acts and recently returned from a successful run as part of a comedy sketch troupe at the Edinburgh Festival. He also writes and directs short films, as well as uploading to his Youtube channel. David can be found on Facebook, Twitter @djthedavid, Instagram @storydj and on Youtube at youtube.com/storydj.

More Books.

<u>Love and Space Dust.</u>

Love & Space Dust is a poetry anthology exploring love and eternity. Timeless poetry of feeling and emotion, Love & Space Dust carries readers on a journey through love, life and relationships, and then far beyond, into the stars and the far flung galaxies, where all that remains of the feelings we once felt and the lives we once lived is love and space dust.

"After spending over ten years in a literature club and hearing/reading more poems than I could count, I thought I had seen it all. I have never been so wrong. Love and Space Dust contains so many beautifully written poems that brought tears to my eyes that I didn't put my Kindle down until I had read every single one of them at least twice." Amazon.de Customer Review.

"Lovely book." Amazon.com Customer Review.

"I really enjoy all of the poems. They make you feel like never before. By far some of my favorite poems." Amazon.com Customer Review.

"LOVED LOVED LOVED THIS!!" Goodreads Review.

"These poems are so full of Pain and Darkness, but so full of Hope and Light." Amazon.de Customer Review.

"This book is absolutely amazing and i hope there will be more to come!" Amazon.com Customer Review.

"Love this book so much!" Goodreads Review.

"Made me smile and moved me to tears." Amazon.co.uk Customer Review.

<u>Could You Ever Live Without?</u>

Poems of feeling and experience, the anthology encompasses all of life and beyond: death, the universe, hopes, dreams, love, loss - all of existence contained in one work. Poetry that captures both moments and lifetimes, memories and hopes, reality and dreams. Poems to identify with, poems of life.

"Take it from a non-poetry reader: this book is a gem, destined to become timeless." Amazon Customer Review.

"Loved the poems, a very great read. Once I started reading it was hard to stop." Amazon Customer Review.

"This book is beautiful. It's one of my most cherished possessions." Amazon Customer Review.

"Not all poetry is worth reading. This is." Amazon Customer Review.

"A great reflection of the deeper thoughts from this generation." Amazon Customer Review.

"Beautiful collection of poetry, I'm not an avid poetry reader but this book is absolutely stunning." Amazon.co.uk Customer Review.

"Everytime I read this book I find new meanings." Goodreads Review.

Love As The Stars Went Out.

A collection of poetry from the end of the world. Poems of love, feeling and emotion, the collection encompasses all of life, and even beyond. Simple and elegant, the book contains all the poetry of existence.

"This book is amazing I would really recommend getting the other two as well they are some of my favourite books of all time." Amazon.co.uk Customer Review.

"I love every bit of this book. So simple yet deep meaningful words. I would recommend it to all and everyone...." Amazon.com Customer Review.

"Five stars. Awesome book." Amazon.com Customer Review.

"Such a beautiful piece." Amazon.com Customer Review.

Death's Door.

"She was like the dawn, insubstantial and somehow transient, as though she would fade from reality at any moment."

Every day the villagers watch as Death, a spectral suit of black armour mounted upon a horse, rides through the valley beneath their mountain top home. After a lifetime living on the edge of Death's domain, his close proximity is neither terrible or threatening, rather he has become a simple fact of life and a familiar neighbour. Nothing seems to change until one night a young boy, alone in the meadows beneath a summer moon, watches a mysterious figure in white approaching the village through the tall grass.

"A spectacular novella, a quick read but engaging and thoughtful. The story carries you as swift as death's horse does." Amazon.com Customer Review.

"Buy this book! Great teen-based book. Even better for post teen (aka 55 year old father) reader." Amazon.com Customer Review.

"This book quickly became my forever favourite. You will not regret buying it. Although it's about death himself, it has so much to teach about life." Amazon.com Customer Review.

Moonlight & You.

"You were never my dream to dream."

Moonlight And You is not only about dreams, but what remains of those dreams after the dawn, and what is left of our wildest hopes, our most vivid fantasies and our fairytale loves. The book explores themes of love, relationships, heartbreak and loss but also hope, and the search for happiness. Its setting is ethereal night's beneath the moon, when time stands still and anything in the world seems possible.

Moonlight And You blurs the boundaries between love, dreams and reality. It delves into our dreams, and how we might hold onto them after the embers of the dawn.

"I love this book! Beautiful read. Five stars." Amazon Customer Review.

Highway Heart.

Highway Heart is a collection of over one hundred poems on relationships, life and the universe. The theme is journeys - the travel we undertake in life, the type of internal travel which traces roads inside our hearts.

Half an exploration of the difficulties of finding the right path in life, and half a bitter sweet celebration of the myriad of strange, exciting, heartbreaking and unexpected roads we discover for ourselves, Highway Heart is above all else the poetic tale of a journey.

"This is one of the greatest works I've ever read. This is truly, truly, a masterpiece. I hope it gets more recognition in the future. Please, please read it, it will touch the deepest parts of your heart." Amazon.com Review.

Loud World, Quiet Thoughts

From the author of the best selling poetry collection Love And Space Dust and the writer behind the internationally famous poetry account @storydj comes a book about love, heartbreak, life - and how to survive all three amongst the noise of our modern world.

Loud World, Quiet Thoughts is divided into two parts. The first consists of short prose, aphorisms and quotes focused on the deafening noise of the modern world; of social media, of television, and pressure. It embodies the endless anxiety of contrasting voices and white noise so loud that it drowns out our own thoughts. The second consists of beautiful poetry drawn from our quietest thoughts and the depths of our souls, thoughts about love and heartbreak and, most of all, hope.

Above all else, Loud World, Quiet Thoughts is a book about reconciling the secret spaces of your heart with the white noise of the world outside.

"I loved all the poems in this book." Amazon.com Review.

The Instagram Writers' Handbook: Beat the Algorithm, Get Followers, Sell Books

There are over 75 million people using the top three writing tags on Instagram. The social network is quickly becoming the go-to platform for writers starting, developing and advancing their career.

Written SPECIFICALLY for writers, the Instagram Writers' Handbook isn't a book that promises to get you a million followers in a month, or skyrocket you to selling a million books per year. Instead, it will teach you how to build a sustainable and realistic career as a writer, growing your follower count each week, increasing your post-by-post engagement and reach, and generating reliable profits through the sale of your books. It will not make you world famous overnight, but it will help you reach your goal of transforming your love of writing into a successful, profitable and long term career.

Beat The Algorithm - The Instagram algorithm controls and often limits who sees your posts, but we can beat it. Increase your post reach, your engagement and over all account health. By using a mixture of post frequency, learning the THREE criteria behind every successful/viral post, using my secret hashtag methods and learning how to build relationships with your followers, you will be able to create an account that the algorithm loves - meaning it will prioritise your posts and show them to more people. Don't pay for paid reach!!

Get Followers - A large follower count is attractive, but useless in the long run unless you are bringing in new followers, new potential customers and new readers. Learn how to reach different, targeted groups of readers, attract only users who are highly engaged and interested in your work, and generate reliable, high numbers of new weekly followers. Don't pay for shoutouts!!

Sell Books - Followers and high engagement are vanity metrics on their own. Learn how to convert your followers into readers, and your likes into sales. I will teach you how to transform a large following into a hyper engaged one, where your followers aren't just numbers, but fans and readers. Don't pay for adverts!!

Starting from zero, the book takes you through every step on your career as an Instagram writer, from creating an effective marketing profile, to publishing your first book, establishing a productive post schedule and ensuring that your posts reach the maximum possible number of readers, and how to convert those readers into customers. It will teach you:

How to publish a book.
The three criteria behind every successful and/or viral piece of content.
How to gain high numbers of daily, new followers.
How to ensure that your posts get high levels of reach and engagement.
How to use hashtags to reach a huge but targeted audience.
My three secret hashtag methods for gaining followers, increasing engagement and making sales.
How to schedule your posts to maximise your profile's effectiveness with the algorithm.
How to reach actual readers, not just unengaged followers.
How to convert ALL of these factors into sales and daily, predictable and sustainable income as an Instagram writer.

The book even includes a list of over 600 of the best writing hashtags, which you can use on your account NOW to beat the algorithm, get followers and sell books.

Learn the methods that have gained me a huge following on Instagram, brought my books to a global audience, seen them featured in the best seller charts on Amazon stores across the world and allowed me to fulfil my dream of making of a profitable career out of the thing I love the most: writing.

"Thank you so much David for sharing this information with your readers. I would have never known of the enormous things that work behind this huge platform had I not grabbed your book. These information are so valuable and I thank you again for sharing this with us." Amazon.com Review.

Printed in Great Britain
by Amazon

85041129R00068